# SAN DIEGO COUNTY VICTORIANS

## TEXT AND PHOTOGRAPHY

### BY

## ERIC C. PAHLKE

## OUR HERITAGE
P · R · E · S · S
SAN DIEGO, CALIFORNIA

Published by Our Heritage Press • 2476 San Diego Avenue • San Diego, CA 92110

ISBN-13 978-0-9800950-0-5
ISBN-10 0-9800950-0-X

Dedicated to Heinz E. Pahlke who bought me my first camera,
Lottie Pahlke for encouraging my early photographic efforts, and
Barbara Pahlke for supporting me in this and everything else I do.

# TABLE OF CONTENTS

# Introduction

San Diego County has a surprising number and diversity of Victorian houses still standing today. Tucked away in older neighborhoods, these houses are a well kept secret.

Several signature homes from the Victorian period have survived. Once the homes of the area's wealthiest residents who entertained the city's high society, these structures are now the offices of lawyers and doctors or are being showcased as bed & breakfast inns. Many remain as residential; some converted to accommodate more than one family unit.

These remaining Victorians are in various states of repair. Some have been restored to their original glory with their ornate woodwork inside and out and vibrant color schemes. Others are barely being maintained, no longer the primary feature of the neighborhood. As you tour areas where these structures still stand, you go from awe at seeing a living example of the Victorian period to a sinking feeling looking at a house that may not be there the next time you drive by.

When I began the research and photography for San Diego County Victorians I wanted to display the diversity of construction, both in design and function, as well as the geographical spread of the Victorian influence. I wanted to use full color because, to me, Victorian means color; not just on the exterior, but on the rich woodwork and intricate wallpapers of their interiors.

I also wanted to show a range of lifestyles during the Victorian period. I have included some of the region's most ornate examples of Victorian architecture such as the Britt-Scripps House, the Long-Waterman House, Villa Montezuma, and the Quartermass-Wilde House, all in San Diego, as well as the Dickinson-Boal House in National City and the Beach House in Escondido. In these homes community leaders lived a fairly pampered life and entertained their contemporaries. These structures were individually designed by the noted architects of their time.

I have also included the houses of the average citizen. Included are houses that were rentals such as those built by J. B. Spaeth and Edward F. French, north of the new downtown San Diego. The Loring House in Golden Hill was probably another rental unit. The book also contains photographs of numerous unnamed houses where the general populace lived. To complete the portrait of the times, you will find several farmhouses including the Gail House in San Marcos and the Stein Farm in National City.

What the reader will not find is a picture of every Victorian house still standing in San Diego County. During the late 19th century development spread across the entire region and many noteworthy houses remain in areas not highlighted in this book, some as close-in as Point Loma and others as far away as Valley Center and Alpine. There is a story for every house and, for those in need of restoration and protection, hopefully, a brighter future ahead.

Without exception, every owner of a restored Victorian wants to talk about their home. They know the history of their house and have many stories of how they lovingly restored them. Perhaps my work to highlight their results will inspire others to undertake the same effort and will allow them to see the benefit of saving these and other historic structures from San Diego County's past.

I hope my photographs do some justice to the beauty of these houses. I want people to get excited about them, visit them, talk to the owners, and become advocates for saving them for generations to come. These houses are not only beautiful, but they speak of the fierce independence of the people who built them in the middle of sagebrush and dust, giving life to a region that would become one of the best places to live in the country.

Eric C. Pahlke
San Diego, California
November 13, 2007

# Are There Victorian Houses in San Diego County?

When people think of Victorian houses on the West Coast, not many think of San Diego. Those who do may recall a newspaper or magazine article about Heritage Park in Old Town San Diego, where Save Our Heritage Organisation (SOHO) and the San Diego County Board of Supervisors were able to relocate several houses before they succumbed to the wrecking ball. Or perhaps they are familiar with the Victorian mansion east of downtown San Diego called Villa Montezuma, a signature building saved by members of SOHO and the San Diego Historical Society.

Instead, they most likely envision San Francisco. For many the classic row houses on Steiner Street across from Alamo Square probably come to mind. Many Californians would be surprised to see the number and diversity of Victorian structures still standing in San Diego County. Most might be more surprised that there are Victorian houses in San Diego that even rival those in cities much better known for them, such as Alameda and San Francisco.

The houses on the following page are typical California Victorians found in San Diego, Alameda, and San Francisco.

Can you guess which ones are located in San Diego County?

Victorian Row Houses – Steiner Street
Alamo Square, San Francisco

Eastlake

Queen Anne #1

Italianate

Queen Anne #2

Queen Anne #3

Answers on page 75

# San Diego County in Victorian Times

The Victorian era is defined as the period of Queen Victoria's reign, from 1837 to 1901. Although San Diego Bay was discovered by Juan Rodriguez Cabrillo in 1542, San Diego was not founded until July 16, 1769 with the establishment of the Royal Presidio de San Diego and the Mission San Diego de Alcalá. There was little development until the early 1800s in what is now called Old Town, the construction mostly confined to adobe structures.

The areas of San Diego County where the majority of Victorian-era structures were built were not subdivided until much later. The city of San Diego was incorporated in 1850, shortly after California became the thirty-first state in the Union. At the time there were approximately 115 structures in the new city. Ten years later the city had an official population of 731 residents.

In 1867, Alonzo Erastus Horton came from San Francisco and shortly thereafter filed a subdivision for what is now downtown San Diego and Bankers Hill. Some early Victorian houses were built in this subdivision, known as Horton's Addition.

The city's population hovered around 2,000 until the building boom of the 1880s, brought about by the completion of the Santa Fe Transcontinental Railroad in November 1885. By 1887 the population was estimated to be as high as 50,000. The boom went bust by 1888 and the population shrunk to 16,000 by the end of the decade. During the Great Boom the county's population also grew more than four fold, reaching almost 35,000 in the 1890 census.

San Diego during the 1890's. Courtesy Coons collection

Much of the growth during this period occurred downtown and to the north and east. Sherman's Addition, now called Sherman Heights, quickly followed Horton's Addition in 1867, and Golden Hill was added around 1872.

Many of the county's largest and most ornate Victorians were built in these two communities and north of downtown, including Bankers Hill, Cleveland Heights, Florence Heights, and Middletown, first mapped in 1870. Houses in these areas boast some of the finest examples of Victorian architecture in the county.

Logan Heights, just south of downtown San Diego, developed during the 1880s and 1890s, and filled in the gap between San Diego and National City to the south. A variety of Victorian era styles is still evident in this community today.

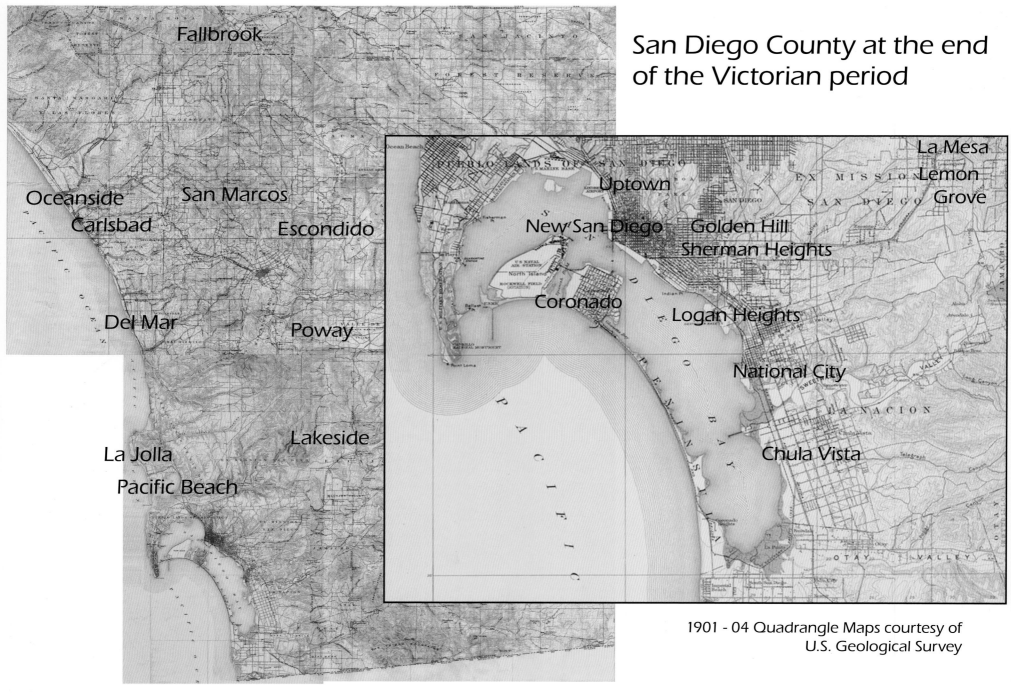

San Diego County at the end of the Victorian period

Fallbrook

Oceanside
Carlsbad
San Marcos
Escondido
Del Mar
Poway
Lakeside
La Jolla
Pacific Beach

La Mesa
Lemon Grove
Uptown
New San Diego
Golden Hill
Sherman Heights
Coronado
Logan Heights
National City
Chula Vista

1901 - 04 Quadrangle Maps courtesy of
U.S. Geological Survey

4

National City was the second city to be incorporated in San Diego County. When it chartered in 1887 it had a population of well over 1,000. Much of the initial development was devoted to raising citrus on 20-acre plots in National City and on five- and ten-acre plots in what was to become Chula Vista, which was incorporated in 1911. Known as orchard houses, some of the Victorians built in these orchards were quite large.

People began to settle in the San Luis Rey Valley to the north of the city of San Diego in the late 1860s and 1870s. Land in what is now downtown Oceanside was plotted in 1885, and the city of Oceanside was incorporated in mid-1888.

To the east, the Spanish rancho Rincon del Diablo (Devil's Corner) passed into the hands of the Wolfskill brothers in 1868 and people began to move into what is now the Escondido Valley. The city of Escondido was incorporated in late 1888 and had a population of 541 residents in the official census two years later.

By 1886, across San Diego Bay from downtown San Diego, the Coronado Beach Company was building a resort community. The world-famous Hotel del Coronado opened for business in February 1888, and the city of Coronado was incorporated in 1890.

Slightly more than half of the county's residents lived within municipal boundaries by 1890. Growth in the 1880s was spreading in all directions, with houses being constructed in what became the cities of Carlsbad, Chula Vista, Del Mar, La Mesa, Lemon Grove, Poway, and San Marcos. A limited number of Victorians were also built in areas that remain unincorporated today, such as Lakeside, Fallbrook, and Valley Center.

Most of the houses constructed in the outlying areas of the county were simple farmhouses, while those

Orchard Homes in National City, circa 1928. Courtesy Peoples/Pro collection

built near the coast were generally beach cottages or summer homes. These houses, with some notable exceptions, were simple structures with less ornamentation.

Population growth in the county slowed dramatically during the 1890s, closing at 35,090 for a net increase of only 103 for the ten-year period. The dawn of the twentieth century saw another growth spurt, but most new houses reflected the Craftsman or Arts and Crafts style. By 1905 there were very few Victorian designs on the drawing board. The Victorian era of house building in San Diego County was over by the time the queen who gave the era its name passed on across the Atlantic.

# Heritage Park, San Diego

Located in Old Town San Diego just southeast of the Old Town San Diego State Historic Park, Heritage Park began to take shape when the County of San Diego moved the Sherman-Gilbert House there in 1971 at the urging of Save Our Heritage Organisation. Soon after, four large houses, a worker's cottage, and the first Jewish temple in San Diego, were saved from demolition and moved to the park. No book about Victorian houses in San Diego County would be complete without a mention of this Victorian Village.

The Sherman-Gilbert House was built in 1887 for John Sherman and sold to the Gilbert family ten years later. The structure exhibits many typical Stick design features, including the large square tower, ornate stickwork expressing the building structure on the outside, irregular rooflines, and stained glass.

The Bushyhead House was also built in 1887. Edward W. Bushyhead was an early San Diego sheriff and one of the first owners of the *San Diego Union* newspaper. The house is in the Eastlake style with its steep roof, detailed wood facing, and squared bay windows with ornate bargeboards.

The McConaughy House was built for John McConaughy in 1887. He started a passenger and freight railroad between San Diego and the mining town of Julian. This structure is an Italianate design inspired by the villas of Italy. The hipped roof, bay windows, and cornice brackets are typical of the style.

Built in 1889, the Christian House was the home of Harfield Timberlake Christian. Over the years he served as alderman, city clerk, and city assessor.

He also sat on the Board of Freeholders that wrote the city of San Diego's initial charter. His house is an example of the Queen Anne style with its round tower, wrap-around porch, bay windows, and shingled second story bargeboards.

The Burton House was built in 1893 in the Colonial Revival style. This was a late Victorian style that recalled the homes of our country's founding.

Located just two blocks to the west of Heritage Park, the Verna House represents another Victorian style that was once prevalent in San Diego County. Built around 1872, this Second Empire structure has a mansard roof with variegated color roof shingles. The 2nd floor dormers are also typical of the style. This house, originally located in downtown San Diego, was moved to Old Town San Diego in 1965.

Bushyhead House (1887)

Burton House (1893)

McConaughy House (1887)

Christian House (1889)

Sherman-Gilbert House (1887)

Verna House (1872)

# New San Diego

When Alonzo Horton arrived in San Diego in 1867, the center of activity was Old Town. On May 10 of that same year he purchased 960 acres approximately three miles to the southeast and filed a subdivision called Horton's Addition. By 1870 the basic street grid that was to become the major portion of today's downtown San Diego had been laid out and a few buildings erected. Horton built a wharf at the foot of Fifth Avenue in 1869, and this became the new town's main street.

There were 2,300 people living in the city of San Diego when Horton laid out his new subdivision. Placer gold was discovered in the mountains outside of Julian in 1880, and the official population reached 2,637. The first transcontinental railroad reached San Diego in 1885.

Most of the surviving Victorians in downtown San Diego were built during the 1880s. Several started out as rental units. One of these is the Italianate 2-story house built on the north edge of present-day downtown by Clawson Jones.

Clawson Jones Rental (1887) 1658 Front Street

Wharf on San Diego Bay, circa 1890's. Courtesy Coons collection

Ordway-Cassidy House (1888) 1620 Union Street

The single-story Queen Anne style cottage above is one of the smaller Victorian remaining in the downtown area. The detailing on the gable and over the porch as well as the spindle work on the porch is typical of the style. The Ordways and Cassidys were two of its earliest occupants.

The Eastlake house on the right was built as a rental and stands two blocks to the east on State Street. The flat roof with cornice brackets and the squared bay windows are very typical of this style. It was constructed in 1888 by J. B. Spaeth, an early contractor. His own residence, which he built next door, has been extensively remodeled over the years.

J.B. Spaeth Rental (1888) 1642 State Street

This Stick style cottage stands two lots to the north of the Ordway-Cassidy House. The treatment on the gables and detailing of the entryway cover are typical of this style. This two-story house was originally another rental unit built by Edward F. French.

The large Victorian house along the north edge of downtown on 3rd Avenue was the home of numerous prominent early families. At the time it was constructed it had a view of downtown San Diego and the bay to the south. Now referred to as the McCormick–Christian House it was also home to the Harfield and Timberlake families.

The projecting bay windows, irregular rooflines, band of shingles, and ornate chimney are characteristic of the Queen Anne style.

Edward F. French Rental (1888) 1654 Union Street

McCormick-Christian House (1893) 1916 3rd Avenue

Dr. F. C. Sheldon had a house built at the corner of 11th Street and D Street (now Broadway) in 1886. The house was designed by Comstock and Trotsche, the same firm that designed Villa Montezuma. Although the house was built for his wife and nine children, Sheldon never lived in it. He caught pneumonia while on a cruise down the Mexican coast celebrating the completion of his signature residence. The first social event to take place in Sheldon's house was his funeral. Left without the means to support herself, Mrs. Sheldon turned the property into a successful boarding house. She later moved the house to its present location at 1245 Island Avenue in 1913.

The Sheldon House is an excellent example of the Queen Anne style of Victorian architecture. The bay windows, multiple rooflines, wrap-around porch, elaborate shingles, and spindle work are all typical Queen Anne. The house was constructed with a redwood exterior and a Douglas fir frame, referred to as Oregon pine. The front door has a decorative design cut into the redwood. Porch ceilings were usually painted light blue to give a feeling of being open to the sky.

Sheldon House  (1886) 1245 Island Avenue

The two-story Queen Anne on the corner of 6th Avenue and Beech Street was built for Dr. W. Peper in 1894. The corner entrance and parapet are distinguishing features of this house.

This Italianate style home was constructed in 1894 by Charles Kiessig. He came to San Diego in 1886 and was active in real estate as well as owning a gun shop. The hipped roof, bay windows, decorative porch woodwork, and cornice brackets are characteristics of the Italianate style. The two-story side porch was probably not part of the original construction. This design style was typically built much earlier in the Victorian period. The house stayed in the family for 82 years. Standing in stark contrast to the skyscrapers that define the area today, it is the closest Victorian structure to City Hall.

Dr. W. Peper Residence (1894) 1502 6th Avenue

Kiessig House (1894) 1407 2nd Avenue

# Sherman Heights

In June 1867 Matthew Sherman bought 160 acres of land east of downtown San Diego for grazing his sheep. Later that year he subdivided his parcel as Sherman's Addition. The development of this area paralleled activity in Horton's Addition to the east and Golden Hill to the north during the last two decades of the 19th century.

One of the boom era Victorian structures in Sherman Heights is the Stuyck House, built in 1887. Prominent architect and builder Thomas J. Armstrong and his family lived in the house during the late 1890s. The house was sold to Wealthy A. McNabb and Henry W. McNabb in 1899. The side staircase was added later. William Hollington built a large Queen Anne house, very similar in design to the Stuyck House, on the corner of L and 21st Streets in 1887.

Stuyck House (1887) 542 21st Street

Hollington House (1887) 171 21st Street

Both houses have the multiple rooflines and tall windows characteristic of the Queen Anne style. The ridge cresting and Anglo-Japanese railing are also distinguishing features. There were at least four homes built using this plan in the area.

Villa Montezuma (1887) 1925 K Street

One of the best-known Victorians in San Diego, Villa Montezuma, is also the most architecturally unusual house built during the period. The design is quintessential Queen Anne, characterized by the numerous patterns of decorative shingles covering the house and towers. The house also exhibits a lack of symmetry and has windows of varying sizes and designs.

The house was built in 1887 on land donated by William High to lure the world-famous concert pianist Benjamin Jesse Francis Shepard to the developing town. Shepard lived in the home for only two years, then sold the house when the land boom of the 1880s turned to bust in 1890.

The house is painted in its original colors described in *The San Diego Union* as a somber collection of harmonious colors, hardly what we might call it today. An 1887 advertisement for Sherwin Williams touted this same scheme as perfect for the Queen Anne house.

This Eastlake house, built in 1888, was owned by Elizabeth Armstrong, widow of William Armstrong of the grocery Monahan & Armstrong. The second-story side door and staircase were later additions.

Armstrong House (1888) 117-19 20th Street

The Sherman–Hearns House is a fairly simple two-story Queen Anne house with half sunbursts on its gables, a very popular treatment of the time.

Sherman–Hearns House (1887) 633 20th Street

Another Queen Anne house is located a few blocks away at 404 24th Street. The bay windows and circular attic windows are distinctive. The second story porch was enclosed at a later date.

In 1884, George Journeay became somewhat of a local hero when a torrential rainstorm washed out telegraph lines northwest of the city. He propped up the poles and restrung the lines only to have them again washed out. Undaunted, he went out and strung the lines a second time. Journeay built his Queen Anne house on the corner of 20th and G Streets around 1895.

404 24th Street

Journeay House (c. 1895) 670 20th Street

A retired local attorney, W. C. Howard, and his wife Mary built their Queen Anne home on 20th Street north of Market Street in 1889. The house was constructed with gables over every one of the upstairs windows. The sunburst design was featured in the gables as well as the corners of the arched front windows. The bay windows are a distinguishing feature. The entryway porch has since been enclosed. Howard died just a few years after they occupied the house; Mary Howard purchased the lot to the north and built a Colonial Revival apartment building for additional income.

W.C. Howard, Esq. House (1889) 657 20th Street

John and Lillie Crellin built their home on 20th Street in 1887. A fine example of Stick Eastlake, the home was sold to Mary Howard in 1900 and used as a rental. The fanlight in the front gable is a distinguishing feature. This cottage and the Howard house to the north were originally built on the same lot and have a common owner even today.

Crellin Cottage (c. 1887) 651 20th Street

# Golden Hill

Golden Hill developed north of Sherman Heights and south and east of City Park (now Balboa Park). The first land transaction there took place in 1872, but the area only began to develop fifteen years later.

The local residents planted and maintained Golden Hill Park in the southeastern corner of what would become Balboa Park. They had to bring the water in by buckets because there was no local source. One of the city's first golf courses was built in this park. Golden Hill has panoramic views of San Diego Bay to the west and was for many years the most fashionable place to live in the city. Today, it is experiencing a Renaissance with many historic homes being restored.

In 1887 Albert M. Hayward built an Eastlake house east of the developing downtown of San Diego. At the time, Hayward was the captain of the yacht *San Diego*. He later sold the house to Francis Elliot Patterson, an early San Diego photographer. Patterson had served in the army as a first lieutenant at the San Diego Mission in 1851. His photos are a large part of the photographic collection of the San Diego Historical Society. The house stayed in the family until 1968.

This house has a flat roof, cornice brackets, tall bay windows, and shingles over the porch and first-floor windows, all characteristic features of the style. The sunroom over the front porch was enclosed sometime after the original construction.

Hayward-Patterson House (1887) 2148 Broadway

Loring House (1893) 2140-44 F Street

1930 30th Street (1887)

The Loring House is an Italianate style structure built in 1893. The hipped roof and latticework are typical of the style. The ridge cresting is a characteristic of the Victorian period. This house may have originally been built as a rental unit.

The Second Empire or French Mansard house at 1930 30th Street was moved in 1910 from downtown at 7th and A Streets, and is one of only four houses of this popular style of the period remaining in the city of San Diego.

The Queen Anne residence at 2026 East Broadway has been beautifully restored. Characteristics of the style are seen in its peak-roofed tower, steep roof, and shingled gables. The iron ridge cresting on the main roof is another distinguishing feature.

2026 East Broadway

Falk-Klauber House (1888) 3000 E Street

M. D. Falk built his Italianate style house in 1888, using redwood from his own sawmill. He sold the house to Abraham Klauber in 1892. Klauber was a partner in one of the city's largest wholesale grocery firms. He expanded the house over the years by approximately one-third, keeping with the original design. At the time of its construction this house was on the very edge of the San Diego urbanized limit in an area known as Coyoteville.

Although the stone wall surounding the front of the house is original, the tower has been recreated. The arched upper-story windows are often seen with this style. The house also features its original patterned redwood doors and window seats. The outside staircase was built later when the house was converted to multifamily use.

Irving Gill's first commission in San Diego was this Colonial Revival house built in 1893 for Daniel Schuyler, one of the city's first park commissioners, who lived in Golden Hill for fifty years. The narrow siding, bay windows, and columns are characteristic of the Colonial Revival style. The incompatible upper porch railing is to be replaced by the current owner.

Schuyler House (1893) 838 25th Street

Quartermass-Wilde House (1896) 2404 East Broadway

Early developer and department store owner Reuben Quartermass built this Queen Anne house with Colonial Revival features directly east of downtown San Diego in 1896. Eleven years later, he built the Quartermass-Stensrud house, a two-story Colonial style hipped-roof cottage near present-day San Diego State University.

The house later passed to Louis J. Wilde. In 1909, Wilde donated the Irving Gill-designed Broadway Fountain that was saved from demolition and still stands in front of Horton Plaza, and in 1912, he was instrumental in having the street in front of his property changed from D Street to Broadway. In 1917, Wilde ran a successful mayorial campaign against George Marston, in which the central issue was "smokestacks vs. geraniums." Wilde, whose slogan was "More Smokestacks," nicknamed his opponent "Geranium George", implying that Marston favored beauty over industry. Wilde served as mayor of San Diego until 1921.

The dome on the tower was a late addition with its curved windows and shingled skin. The tall windows and unique corner entrance are distinguishing features of this late Victorian house. The curved bay windows are another striking feature.

The Quartermass-Wilde House was restored in 1975.

McKee House (1887) 2460 B Street

841-45 20th Street

Clark McKee built his house in the same year as Albert Hayward a few blocks away. McKee started the first abstract and title company in San Diego, and his wife served on the women's board for the 1915 Panama-California Exposition. This Colonial Revival features a peak-roofed circular Queen Anne tower with curved windows, bay windows, and cornice brackets. The Doric columns on the porch and recessed window in the front gable are in the Colonial Revival style.

The Queen Anne at 841-45 20th Street shares its basic design with the Stuyck and Hollington houses in Sherman Heights. The treatment of the front gable and porch are almost exact copies of each other.

# UPTOWN

The areas north of downtown San Diego began to develop a few years after Horton subdivided the area. Part of what today is called the Uptown area, the subdivisions of Middletown, Florence Heights, and Cleveland Heights were considered an appropriate distance from the bustling New San Diego, situated along the bay front at the Fifth Avenue wharf, for the construction of stylish residences.

In 1868, 1,400 acres of land adjacent to Horton's Addition were set aside for a park; called City Park, it later became Balboa Park. The area to the west of Horton's Addition was subdivided as Middletown in 1870. The land lay dormant until the 1880s.

W. W. Bowers subdivided land north of Grape Street in 1883 as Florence Heights. The surrounding area is now known as Banker's Hill, generally the area from Date Street north to Upas Street. In 1892, streetcars came to Banker's Hill, providing the impetus for the construction of many of the large Victorian houses that still remain today.

Daniel Cleveland arrived in San Diego in 1869 and laid out Cleveland Heights in an area north of Walnut Street in what is today the Hillcrest community. Cleveland was one of the founders of San Diego's first hospital and was involved in the formation of many civic organizations that still exist.

John Sherman, a cousin of General William Tecumseh Sherman, built this house in the Stick style just north of downtown on Fir Street in 1887. Dr. John Rankin Doig bought the house in 1888. Doig had moved from Ellsworth, Kansas in 1886 and had his offices at 4th and C Streets. In 1898 he returned to Kansas to serve as a traveling surgeon for the Union Pacific Railroad. Sherman also built the Sherman-Gilbert House in 1887, which was later saved from demolition and relocated to Heritage Park in Old Town.

Sherman-Doig House (1887) 136 Fir Street

The Torrance House was originally the home of Elisha Swift Torrance, an attorney in early San Diego. Torrance was first elected to the Superior Court in 1890 and served for 18 years. Alonzo Horton lived in the house at one time.

The stained glass windows are original. The open arched gables, tall bay windows, and shingle skirting are distinguishing features of this Queen Anne.

Judge Torrance House (1887) 136 Juniper Street

George James Keating and his wife Fannie had an asymmetrical Queen Anne house built in 1888. For health reasons, they moved in 1886 to San Diego from Kansas City, where his agricultural implement business had grown to be one of the largest in the world, making him a multi-millionaire. Keating invested heavily in the city's booming real estate market. He died unexpectedly in June 1888. The shingle panels, ornate latticework, and sunburst pattern on the entryway gable highlight the Queen Anne style. The hexagonal turret in the rear of the structure is difficult to see from the street. The house has four fireplaces and twelve-foot ceilings.

Hunsaker House (c 1887) 110 Juniper Street

The Hunsaker House was built in 1887 on Juniper Street. William J. Hunsaker served as district attorney for the county of San Diego and was Wyatt Earp's attorney in Tombstone. As lifelong friends, Earp must have visited this house many times and Hunsaker was a pallbearer at his funeral. In 1887 Hunsaker was mayor of San Diego and later became the Dean of the Los Angeles Bar Association; his father was an early sheriff in San Diego. Although an addition in the rear is painted in the same colors as the main building, it does not exhibit any Victorian design features.

George Keating Residence (1888) 2331 2nd Avenue

In 1887, Eugene Britt finished his Queen Anne house, one of the most expensive and lavish residences built in San Diego at the time. Britt was a successful water rights attorney, served on the Supreme Court Commission, and was a California delegate to the Republican National Convention in 1916.

In 1896 E. W. Scripps, owner of the *San Diego Sun* and the *United Press*, and his family purchased the property as their family town home, while also building a ranch in the Miramar area in what was to become the community of Scripps Ranch. The Scripps family entertained the upper crust of San Diego society at their Maple Street residence.

The shingle siding, peaked-roof tower, decorated gables, wrap-around porch, and latticework are defining features of the style. The house was painstakingly restored in 1979, including the interior with its ornate woodwork, lighting, and wallpaper. The exterior is painted in its original colors except for the roof, which would have been terracotta.

The stained glass windows on the west side of the house, along the main staircase, are arguably the most beautiful examples remaining of the craftsmanship of the Victorian era.

Britt-Scripps House (1887) 406 Maple Street

*Britt-Scripps House (1887) 406 Maple Street*

John Long, president of the Coronado Fruit Package Company, built his Queen Anne home on 1st Avenue in 1889. The style is easily identified by its conical tower, corbeled chimneys, curved bay windows, wrap-around porch, and ornate latticework. The extensive use of shingle siding is another distinguishing feature.

Long's wife died shortly after they moved into the house and he sold it to Robert Whitney Waterman, Governor of California from 1887 to 1891. Waterman had made his fortune while living in San Bernardino and owned a silver mine in Barstow. He bought and developed the Stonewall Gold Mine in Cuyamaca where he also owned a cattle ranch. Waterman helped build the San Diego, Cuyamaca, and Eastern Railroad.

Later purchased by Dr. Alfred and Mrs. Florence Gilbert, the house was occupied by sisters Bess and Gertrude Gilbert, who later lived together in the Sherman-Gilbert House now located in Heritage Park in Old Town.

Long - Waterman House   (1889) 2408 1st Avenue

The Moore House was built for a couple from Pennsylvania who retired to San Diego in 1893. This Queen Anne style with Eastlake ornamentation was built with an octagonal tower that originally looked out on almost barren hillsides and canyons as well as San Diego Bay, Coronado, and Point Loma. The wrap-around porch, latticework, and tall windows are typical of the style. The raised porch is uncommon in San Diego.

3551 Front Street (1893)

These two houses north of downtown and west of Balboa Park are San Diego's best representation of the Shingle style. A derivation of the Queen Anne, this uniquely American style, sometimes described as a maturation of the style, incorporates shingle siding into the design and was popular on the East Coast.

2425 1st Avenue

2139 1st Avenue

The house above has an unusual second-story corner support and a variety of unique window designs. The third-story balcony is another distinguishing element.

The house on the left has several unique features, including the recessed dormer window and bay windows on the first two floors. The second-story balcony was probably not enclosed originally.

# LOGAN HEIGHTS

Developed during the mid-1880s and 1890s, Logan Heights was named after Army Major General John A. Logan. Many historians consider him the premier volunteer general of the Civil War.

People were initially drawn to the area in anticipation of a transcontinental railroad terminal being built. Although the depot was eventually built in downtown San Diego, people still came to Logan Heights because of its fertile soil, ocean views, level ground, and proximity to downtown.

The streets were laid out in a northwesterly to southeasterly direction to bring sunshine into every room of every house at some time during the day. Many of the streets are named after military figures, including General Stephen W. Kearny, who fought in the Battle of San Pasqual during the Mexican-American War.

Gorham House (c. 1894) 2042 Kearney Avenue

2084 Kearney Avenue

The Gorham House was built by Cornelius Gorham, a local building contractor. It features one of the few examples of original iron ridge cresting in San Diego. The Queen Anne style can be see in its extensive use of shingle siding and two-story tower.

The Queen Anne cottage a few houses down from the Gorham House was typical of residences occupied by the working class citizens of the time. It was part of a group of what we would today call model homes, built by one developer in the 1890's all along Kearney Avenue. Out of the five or six built, four remain.

The Queen Anne house on South 32nd Street has a raised foundation and sits on a knoll. Its character defining features are expressed in its square two-story tower, porch latticework, and shingle siding on the second-story. When it was first constructed there were very few other buildings in the area, and it probably had very good views to the south and west.

Exchange House (c. 1885) 1851 Irving Avenue

729 South 32nd Street (c. 1895)

The Italianate on Irving Avenue was originally built in Coronado and later ferried across the bay to its present location. The house has been modified numerous times. The square tower and tall bay windows are distinguishing features. The treatments over the bay windows and entryway are also typical. The addition over the side porch was added later, detracting from its original lines.

# PACIFIC BEACH

The community of Pacific Beach was first subdivided in 1887. By 1888 a railroad line connected the new community to Old Town and San Diego. In 1899 Pacific Beach had 100 permanent residents. There are very few examples of Victorian architecture left in this part of San Diego.

Victor Hinkle, a lemon grower, built his house in 1892 in the midst of a lemon grove on Chalcedony Street. It was moved to its current location in 1930. Its Midwestern architectural style reflects Mr. Hinkle's origins in Kansas. The house exhibits Queen Anne features with its square tower, first-floor bay window, and wrap-around porch. The shingle siding and latticework are also typical for the period. The Gothic windows in the tower are recent additions.

Hinkle House (1892) 1576 Law Street

# La Jolla

Opinions are divided on the derivation of La Jolla's name. Some believe that it comes from the Spanish phrase "la joya" meaning "the jewel." Others think that it is derived from the Indian word "oholle" meaning "hole in the mountains."

Although the lands of La Jolla were part of the city of San Diego when it was incorporated in 1850, there were no permanent settlers in the area until 1869. Two brothers, Daniel and Samuel Sizer, purchased 80-acre plots located near the present-day intersection of Fay Street and La Jolla Boulevard. Frank Botsford came to San Diego in 1886 and also purchased a plot for development, which he then subdivided and auctioned off in parcels.

In the 1890s, a railroad line was extended to the town and real estate developers began marketing resort property along the La Jolla coast. An important artist colony, the Green Dragon Colony, developed here, and newspaper heiress and philanthropist Ellen Browning Scripps settled here as well. By 1900 the town had 350 residents.

Villa Waldo, a simple Queen Anne on Drury Lane, was built in 1892 as a multifamily unit, probably for rental purposes in this resort community. The shingle siding and clipped corners are the most prominent Victorian features of an otherwise plain house. The two dormers were probably added at a later date.

Villa Waldo (1892) 7849 Drury Lane

# NATIONAL CITY

Frank Kimball and his brothers Warren and Levi bought El Rancho de la Nación in 1868. They plotted the town of National City next to San Diego Bay and began marketing it with the slogan "Bay and Climate."

Frank Kimball built the first home in the city in 1869, which was located near 10th Street and National Avenue, later renamed National City Boulevard. His house reflected the flat roof and cornices typical of the Italianate style and was distinguished by its indoor plumbing. This house was the centerpiece of social life in National City for many years. Kimball used the extensive grounds that surrounded the house for agricultural experiments including his introduction of olives to the region. The house is now in Heritage Square. The Craftsman porch was added in the early 1900s.

Charles Blossom House (c. 1879) 907 A Avenue

Elizur Steele built his house in 1879 and sold it to the Blossom family in 1883. The tower is typical Queen Anne and was carefully built to a smaller scale so that the house would appear taller. The house was moved from its original location to Heritage Square in 1977. This house appears on the official logo for National City.

Frank Kimball House (1869) 921 A Avenue

40

Dickinson-Boal House (1887) 1433 East 24th Street

This Queen Anne farmhouse was constructed on N Avenue in 1896 for Oliver Noyes, National City's first postmaster. The house sits on a seven-acre parcel of land and probably had clear views to the south and west when it was built. The corner entrance and wrap-around porch are typical design elements. The iron ridge cresting was recreated.

Oliver Noyes House (1896) 2525 N Avenue

One of the finest homes in the county was built for Colonel William G. Dickinson in 1887. The Queen Anne house was designed by the architectural firm of Comstock and Trotsche, the same firm that designed Villa Montezuma. The hexagon tower, wrap-around porch, tall bay windows, and corbelled chimneys, along with its gabled windows and patterned treatments are distinguishing features. Colonel Dickinson was a professional planner and business manager for the San Diego Land and Town Company. He and Frank Kimball were the driving force in building the Sweetwater Dam, which was completed in 1888. Dickinson laid out the community of Chula Vista.

Photo of Frank Kimball and W.G. Dickinson. Courtesy of the Chula Vista Public Library, Local History collection

Known as Brick Row, these ten individual row houses were built by Frank Kimball in 1887 for executives of the Santa Fe Railroad. Designed by R. C. Ball, who also designed Folsom Prison, they are of a style more commonly seen in eastern cities. Each unit has two fireplaces downstairs and four bedrooms upstairs. The front doors open to an imposing oak staircase and the dividing walls on the porch provide privacy. These row houses are on their original site and have been surrounded by other historic homes that were moved to Heritage Square to save them from demolition.

Ira Floyd House (1881) 1941 Highland Avenue

Ira Floyd brought his family to the area in 1876 from New England. He first built a barn on the acreage where they lived until he built an Italianate house in 1881. Although he previously owned a shoe factory he became a fruit rancher. His daughter Carrie painted watercolors of the flora which have been preserved as a record of the beautiful wildflowers that grew in the surrounding countryside more than 100 years ago.

Brick Row (1887) 906-40 A Avenue

A. E. Evans House (1887) 437 G Avenue

Rice purchased lots in National City from the San Diego Land and Town Company in late 1887 and built an Eastlake house at 1311 Roosevelt Avenue, probably for speculation. Little is known of the Proctor family who first occupied the house. The Rice-Proctor House was moved to Heritage Square in 1978. The roof cornices with vertical supports and tall windows are characteristic of the Stick style.

The A.E. Evans House was built in early 1887 by Elizur Steele, a real estate developer and contractor. Ann Evans and her husband Edward had come to National City to farm. This house is an example of Italianate architecture, with its widow's walk, cornices, and tall windows.

Elizur Steele and his brother John built many of the early houses in National City. Steele Canyon is named after the family.

Julius A. Rice was a teacher in the 1870s who also served his whole career as an educator, principal and, later, member of the National City school board. He also sat on the San Diego County school board and served as principal in the city of San Diego. He married John B. Steele's daughter, Laura in 1880 and they lived with the Steele family for several years. They built their own house along 2nd Street in 1887. That house is no longer standing.

Rice-Proctor House (c. 1887) 939 A Avenue

Many of the houses built in San Diego during Victorian times were constructed on knolls, and there are several examples of this practice in National City. Today these houses are encircled by others built on lots derived from the original larger parcel.

The Queen Anne structure built for Moses Kimball sits on just such a knoll, surrounded by trees. It is visible from several directions and has views of downtown San Diego, Point Loma, and the Coronado Islands. The house was the second structure on the same property. The upstairs closet doors, hardware, and fireplace mantel are from the first house. Like the Frank Kimball house, this house had an inside bathroom. In addition, rainwater was collected from the roof and pumped to a holding tank on the roof. The three-story tower, widow's walk, wrap-around porch, and shingle siding are characteristic of the Queen Anne style.

Moses Kimball House (1893) 2202 East 10th Street

Moses Kimball House, circa 1900-10.
Photo courtesy Coons collection

The Moses Kimball House features a three-story staircase and replica period wallpaper on the first floor. There are four sets of pocket doors, dividing the front and back parlors, the entry, and the dining room. The woodwork in the entry hall is golden oak. The rest of the house has fir floors and redwood trim. Although there were no stained glass windows in the house, the diamond pattern window frames are distinctive.

Charles Stein came to the area in 1888 from Germany. His original homestead was in a portion of the county that would be flooded by the Lower Otay Dam in 1897. Stein purchased ten acres at the corner of 18th Street and F Avenue and became a successful teamster and house moving contractor. He married Bertha Pallas in 1891 and they raised five children on the family farm. The Steins were active members of the community and Charles was elected constable during this time period.

The Stein Family Farm, which includes the original house, barn, and attached out buildings, is the last cohesive remnant of a farmstead in the city of National City and is open to the public as a living history museum. The home is painted in its original colors and is a fine example of Victorian vernacular architecture. Many of the furnishings are original and much of the equipment that Stein used in his trucking and house moving business has been preserved. The original barn is a rarity, as most of San Diego County's barns have been lost.

The property is managed by the National City Living History Farm Preserve as a museum, showing what life was like for the common citizens in Victorian times.

Stein Farm (c. 1900). Courtesy Stein Family Farm Museum

Stein Farm, 1808 F Avenue

David K. Horton was one of the largest stockholders in the San Diego Land and Town Company. Originally from Boston, Horton was lured to National City by a letter from Frank Kimball stating, "You will get more comfort living here for 10 years than a life-time in any other place." Horton was not in very good health so he moved his family to the area and began building his house in 1895.

Horton selected a young architect that would later be quite prominent in San Diego, Irving J. Gill. Gill designed a spacious 14-room Colonial Revival structure sitting on five acres just north of the orchard house built for Colonel William G.

Dickinson. The Horton parcel was planted with mostly citrus trees to the west and exotic fruit trees to the east.

The house features a large reception hall with fireplace and wide stairs leading to a railed balcony half-way to the second floor, all constructed of clear heart redwood. The curved fireplace shares the chimney with fireplaces in the parlor and dining room. When it was completed in 1896 the house was equipped with all the most modern conveniences including electrical wiring, indoor plumbing, a kitchen skylight, and central heating provided by three coal-burning furnaces in the cellar.

Horton died a few years after the house was completed. The family lived in the house for several years, but eventually moved back to Boston. The house passed through numerous families until 1919 when Henry C. Keisel, Sr. purchased it. The Keisel family lived in the house until 1983 when the current owner bought it.

Although the house faces north the entry to the property was originally along a palm tree lined driveway from N Avenue to the west. A few of these century-old trees remain on the property.

D.K. Horton House, circa 1900. Courtesy Peoples/Pro collection

D.K. Horton House (1896)  1504 East 22nd Street

# CHULA VISTA

Chula Vista was founded in the late 1880s by the San Diego Land and Town Company, a corporation formed by the Atchison, Topeka, and Santa Fe Railroad. The town was laid out by Colonel William G. Dickinson, who built his home in neighboring National City. By the end of 1887 forty homes were either completed or under way. The construction of the Sweetwater Dam in 1888 ensured a reliable water supply for the new town and agriculture in this part of the county.

James Madison Johnson brought his family to the area from New Hampshire in 1888. Johnson built a house on F Street, and planted a lemon orchard on the rest of his five-acre lot. He became a well-known orchard grower and invented the lemon-washing machine. The house is a simple Stick Victorian.

Haines-Cordrey House (1888) 210 Davidson Street

James Johnson House (1888) 525 F Street

Alfred Haines was an attorney and judge. A recognized authority on water issues, he argued the Chula Vista water rate case before the U. S. Supreme Court in 1900. He sold his house on Davidson Street in 1919 to Hancil Cordrey, a carpenter who created and produced hardware specialties. The three-story tower, corbeled chimney, and roof cornices are characteristic of the Queen Anne style. The front porch was later extended to the sides of the house.

The Maude House was probably built around 1889 for Mrs. B. K. Maude, who called her home and the surrounding ten acres the El Enjambre Ranch (Spanish for "swarm of bees"). It is known locally as the "Boarding House." The original siding has been covered with modern siding.

Although the house at 644 2nd Avenue was apparently constructed in 1888, it sat vacant for twenty years. Its first recorded owners were William and Jennie MacDonald who came from Leavenworth, Kansas, and purchased it on June 8, 1908. The subdivision map that included this lot had been filed by the San Diego Land and Town Company just four days earlier.

Jennie MacDonald traveled extensively and brought back many exotic botanicals. A severe frost in later years killed all the plants except the Chinese Wisteria, which still thrives. The house is classed as a Four-Square Transitional with an open floor plan. The front parlor has a large bay window and pocket doors opening into the music room.

Maude House (c. 1889) 155 G Street

MacDonald House (1888) 644 2nd Avenue

Photo of a typical orchard home built in Chula Vista in the late 1880s. *Courtesy Chula Vista Public Library, Local History collection.*

The Bronson House was probably built around 1888. The first record of it was a story in the *San Diego Union* in 1890 describing it as "one of the finest houses in Chula Vista." There are no official records of the house until Byron and Emma Bronson purchased it from the San Diego Land & Town Company in 1907. The tower with the conical roof is the most distinctive feature of the house. The tall windows, large porch, and shingle siding are also typical of the Queen Anne style. The house is known locally as the "Blue Castle."

Photo courtesy Coons collection

Bronson House (c. 1900)

Bronson House (c. 1888) 613 2nd Avenue

Garrettson House (1889) 642 2nd Avenue

Garrett A. Garrettson was one of the early businessmen to purchase land in the new town of Chula Vista in 1886. He purchased a five-acre lot from the San Diego Land & Town Company and built a Queen Anne house at 166 3rd Avenue in 1889. Garrettson invested heavily in the real estate market. He became one of the largest stockholders, vice president, and a director of the First National Bank, San Diego's oldest bank, and was one of the wealthiest men in San Diego County in his time. This Queen Anne house originally had two parlors, separated by pocket doors. The exterior features three different, scalloped shingle designs, all in California redwood. The house was relocated to the rear of the MacDonald House property in 1982.

Stained glass panel over the parlor window.

A Queen Anne Victorian was built in 1895 for Alvina and Edward Gillette on a promontory with a commanding view of the Sweetwater Valley below. They had arrived from Kenesaw, Nebraska a year earlier. The large three-story tower is a distinguishing feature of the house; the second-story porch was extended at a later date. The house was originally surrounded by citrus orchards.

Gillette House (1895) 44 North 2nd Avenue

# OCEANSIDE

In the late 1860s and 1870s people began to settle in the San Luis Rey Valley, forty miles north of the city of San Diego. These initial settlements were concentrated around the original Spanish Mission, San Luis Rey de Francia. The railroad line was extended from San Diego through Fallbrook to Colton. The city of Oceanside was incorporated in mid-1888, after the railroad was extended to Barstow in 1885, thereby completing the Transcontinental Railroad and touching off the boom of the eighties.

Built one block from the Pacific Ocean, the Henry Graves Residence was built as a resort beach cottage in 1887. This house also served as the flight instructor's house in the 1986 movie *Top Gun*. Graves' main home was on a citrus ranch in Redlands connected by train to Oceanside.

Henry Graves Residence (1887)
102 North Pacific Street

Henry Graves Residence, circa 1887.
Courtesy Coons collection

Sledge Residence (1886) 325 South Ditmar Street

Libby-Rush House (1905) 636 Rockledge Street

The Libby-Rush House was constructed by Charles Libby and later occupied by Goldie Rush, a legendary burlesque star who entertained in north San Diego County.

# ESCONDIDO

One of the thirty original Spanish ranchos in San Diego County, where the Escondido Valley is today, was called Rancho Rincón del Diablo, "Devil's Corner." The origin of the name is unclear.

The rancho was acquired by the Wolfskill brothers in 1868, and the valley was known as Wolfskill Plains for several years. The name was changed to Escondido in 1883. The Spanish word means "hidden" and may have been chosen because foothills surround the valley.

By 1886 a town site had been laid out and a branch line of the Santa Fe Railway was extended to it two years later. The city was incorporated in late 1888 and had a population of 541 in the official 1890 census.

The Escondido Land and Town Company built a "model farm" and "model ranch" to demonstrate to prospective buyers what life could be like in the valley. They also built a brick "model house," which still stands west of downtown Escondido on 3rd Avenue. The roof cornices, bay windows, and arched doorways and windows are distinctive design elements.

The house built for Judge J. N. Turrentine in 1886 is believed to be the oldest in Escondido. The design is very simple with only the bay windows and shingles on the gables reflecting the Italianate style.

Turrentine House (1886) 208 East 5th Avenue

"Model House" (1886) 969 West 3rd Avenue

Beach House (1896) 700 South Juniper Street

The house built in 1896 by Albert Beach, a real estate developer, sits much higher than the neighboring properties. When it was constructed it had a commanding view of the Escondido Valley to the north. The Beach House exhibits typical Queen Anne design elements including the wrap-around porch, roof cornices, tall windows, ornate gables, shingle siding, and latticework. The wooden ridge cresting on the roof peaks is quite distinctive and duplicates the original.

The recent restoration of the Beach House is complete even to the planting of Victorian box hedges. Every room has period wallpaper, rugs, furnishings, and lighting fixtures. The house has four bedrooms and three bathrooms as well as two dining areas.

The owners have also created an elaborate landscape including a formal area complete with antique cast iron garden furnishings. The fountain that forms the centerpiece of the Victorian landscape is an exact replica of an original and surrounding it is a box hedge enclosing heirloom variety roses.

The shingle siding on the gables and skirting can best be viewed from the south. The decorative woodwork along the top of the porch as well as the bottom of the gables is a distinctive design element of the Beach House.

Julius Hickok Anderson had a house built on Juniper Street in 1891 in the Queen Anne style. Anderson was a founding member and cashier of the Bank of Escondido. He and his wife Laura raised three sons in the house. Publisher N. Fredrick Hansen purchased the house in 1905. Later that year, his wife Anna Louise Hansen gave a party that was reported to be "one of the most prominent social events that ever took place in the city."

George Thomas Bandy and his wife Susan bought the house in 1913 and lived there for 45 years. They raised their six children in the house. Bandy operated a blacksmith and wheelwright shop for almost 30 years and did most of the ornamental wrought iron work in the houses and churches in the city. He is credited with doing the cowboy andirons in the Will Rogers ranch in Santa Monica.

The Bandy House has an irregular floor plan and looks somewhat similar to the Comstock & Trotsche-designed Timken House, located at 1st Avenue and Laurel Street in San Diego. The house is sometimes called the Anderson House for its original owners or the Conley House for more recent residents.

Bandy-Conley House (1891) 638 South Juniper Street

204 West 8th Avenue

602 South Grape Street

The Shingle style house east of downtown on 8th Avenue has a wrap-around porch and shingle siding on the second-story. The small Victorian on Grape Street exhibits several Eastlake design elements including a hipped roof, tall windows, ornate porch supports, and a widow's walk.

# Coronado

Sebastián Vizcaíno surveyed the territories now known as San Diego and Coronado in the early 17th century, but failed to settle in the area. Coronado remained forgotten until 1846 when Don Pedro Carrillo was issued a land grant for "the island or peninsula in the Port of San Diego." The island changed hands numerous times over the next 39 years until Elisha S. Babcock, Jr., Hampton L. Story, and Jacob Gruendike purchased it in 1885. Babcock invited his brother-in-law, Heber Ingle, and Josephus Collett to become investors and they organized the Coronado Beach Company in 1886.

Within little more than a week, the first ferry between New San Diego and Coronado was running across the bay. By the end of 1886 the company had sold 350 lots. Houses and businesses were soon under construction, and the city was incorporated in 1890.

834 A Avenue

George Foster House  (1887) 577 B Avenue

The small Queen Anne cottage above near downtown Coronado is distinguished by its bay window, large shingled gable, and latticework along the top of the porch.

George Foster was an early executive with the Coronado Beach Company and mayor from 1894 to 1895. He had the Queen Anne house on the left built for his family in 1887. It was designed by the same architects that built the Hotel del Coronado. The bay windows and shingle siding on the second-story are elements characteristic of the style. The first porch was removed and a new door was added.

J.Y. Jackson had a Queen Anne house built in 1888 on the south part of the island. He was the manager of the mineral water company owned by Elisha S. Babcock, Jr., one of the town founders. The three-story square tower is set off at an angle, which was unusual for the time.

The Queen Anne on Adella Avenue was built in 1889 by John Mitchell. David Balch bought the house in 1891 and remodeled it to its current configuration. Balch is best known for deriving potash from kelp during World War I. The large two-story tower, latticework, and shingle siding are characteristic of the style.

Jackson-Ballou House (1888) 279 C Avenue

Balch House (1888) 725 Adella Avenue

Livingston House (1887) 1144 Isabella Avenue

The Livingston House was constructed in 1887 by Edwin Booker for Harriet Morris Livingston at the corner of 24th and J Streets in Sherman Heights. It was relocated by barge across San Diego Bay to Coronado in 1983.

The house has been affectionately named the "Baby del" by its owners for its architectural similarities to the Hotel del Coronado, just a few blocks away. When it was relocated the owners had a room built on the back mirroring the the Hotel del's Crown Room.

The Queen Anne structure on Orange Avenue has a cupola over the main entrance, tall bay windows, and two different patterns of shingle siding. The paint palette is quite simple, as was very typical for the times, and similar to the Baby del.

The Hanson House was built toward the end of the Victorian period with shingle siding and corner brackets. The gable treatment is quite distinctive.

Hutchings House (1888) 773 Orange Avenue

Hanson House (1880's) 1116 Loma Avenue

# Del Mar

In 1882, the railroad connecting San Diego and Colton was built by Santa Fe interests through what is now the city of Del Mar. Theodore Loop and Jacob Shell Taylor, who were in nearby Rancho Peñasquitos, purchased 338 acres and started a new resort town in 1885. Taylor built numerous small houses as well as a train depot, schoolhouse, and water system. A year later he opened the area's first resort, called Casa Del Mar. He built a dance pavilion on the beach and a large swimming pool that went out into the ocean.

The Edelweiss House was one of the first homes in the subdivision, and was built in the Gothic style with a Queen Anne porch that was later enclosed.

The McKay and Crawford-Reed Houses were built by Taylor with his initial development. Built during the period, these beach cottages are a simple interpretation of Victorian era styling.

William McKay House (1885) 227 10th Street

Edelweiss House (1883) 119 10th Street

Crawford-Reed House (1886) 1726 Coast Boulevard

Schutte Home, c. 1900. Courtesy of the Carlsbad City Library

# CARLSBAD

Gerhard Schutte and three friends formed the Carlsbad Land and Water Company in 1886 and founded a new town along the Pacific Coast at an existing railroad station. They considered the local well water similar to the water from the Karlsbad Bohemia Spas, and this led them to name the new town Carlsbad. Schutte built his home in the Queen Anne style in 1887. The circa 1900 photograph shows a circular tower that was a prominent feature in the original design, but now is just one of three towers. Although the structure has been substantially enlarged and altered over the years, the changes were obviously designed to retain the Victorian character of the building. Its shingle siding, roof cornices, and latticework are typical for the period.

Schutte Residence (1887) 2978 Carlsbad Boulevard

# La Mesa

Present-day La Mesa was part of the vast lands of Mission San Diego de Alcalá. In 1869 Robert Allison, a rancher from Vacaville, purchased 4,282 acres out of a 60,000 acre rancho that had been granted to Santiago Argüello, commandant of the Presidio of San Diego. For many years he operated a ranch and rest stop known as Allison Springs.

The San Diego Flume Company brought a reliable water source to the area in 1887. The area's initial growth period began in 1894 when A. S. Crowder and Robert Allison's son Joseph filed the La Mesa Springs subdivision map. Streets were graded and five- and ten-acre lemon orchards planted.

The area remained largely agricultural until 1906, when Sherman Grable and Charles Park formed the Park-Grable Investment Company and developed 200 acres in central La Mesa into 1,000 lots. The community quickly grew to 700, and the city of La Mesa was incorporated in February 1912.

Frank Oliver House (1907) 4657 4th Street

Albert W. Gray House (1891) 8045 Culowee Street

Frank Morris Oliver worked as a cowboy in Colorado before moving to the area. He built an L-shaped Colonial Revival farmhouse on 4th Street in 1907 and is believed to have operated the first nursery. Dr. John H. Mallery, La Mesa's third mayor, lived in the house in later years. The shingled gables are the only Victorian elements evident. The dormers were probably added later.

The Queen Anne cottage built by La Mesa's first postmaster, Albert W. Gray, is thought to be the city's oldest building still standing on its original site. This Victorian cottage has shingles on the gables.

The majority of Victorian-era structures remaining in La Mesa are simple one- and one and a half-story cottages. The cottage on 4th Street is distinguished by bay windows, a three-section gable window, shingle siding, and ornate latticework. The extra gingerbread was added later.

4677 4th Street

# LEMON GROVE

Lemon Grove developed later than neighboring La Mesa because of a lack of water and its not being on a traveled route. The primary activities in the area were sheep and poultry ranching as well as vegetable crops and orchards. Although Lemon Grove is one of the older communities in the county, it wasn't incorporated until 1977. The city is named after the many lemon groves that used to cover the hillsides.

The Parsonage Museum is housed in what was originally the Atherton Chapel, built in 1897. The bell tower was later removed and the structure converted to a single-family residence. The shingle siding and ornamentation along the eaves are Victorian era design elements.

Parsonage Museum 3185 Olive Street

# Poway

Poway's contemporary history began in 1758, when the padres from the Mission San Diego de Alcalá used the valley for cattle grazing. Settlers first came to the area in the late antebellum period. In 1887 about 800 people lived and farmed there.

During the last two decades of the nineteenth century efforts were made to extend a railroad into the town. In 1887 an English firm laid out a subdivision plan called Piermont that envisioned an extensive park system. When the railroad did not materialize, people began to leave the valley.

The Plaisted House is named after the family that homesteaded the property. The porch details were recently added.

Plaisted House (1886) 14221 Midland Road

# San Marcos

Cave Couts purchased part of the original Mexican land grant that is now San Marcos in the late 1850s and raised livestock. John H. Barham started the first town in 1883. In 1887 the San Marcos Land Company bought most of the land from the Couts family and subdivided it into tracts. In that year the Santa Fe Railroad announced plans to lay tracks through the valley. Although the tracks were laid a mile from town, San Marcos was still established by 1896.

The Gall House is one of a handful of Victorian farmhouses still remaining. The porch details are defining features.

Gall House (1895-1901) 1319 Knob Hill Road

# Lakeside

In the late 1890s the sagebrush and cactus in the area of present-day Lakeside were cleared to make room for lemon orchards, vineyards, and a few residences.

The Castle House was built in 1887 by G. H. Mansfield, vice president of the El Cajon Valley Land Company. He built it as a showpiece in the Queen Anne style. The circular tower, shingle siding, and tall windows are typical of the style. The house was originally constructed of redwood and Oregon pine.

When it was constructed, fifty acres of orchards and vineyards surrounded the house, and Mansfield raised grapes for raisins. Situated on the side of a hill, it had a panoramic view of the valley to the north and west. Today the view is obstructed by the surrounding houses built on many of the original fifty acres.

Castle House (1887) 12747 Castle Court Drive

# Fallbrook

In the early 1870s the U.S. government surveyed what was to become the Fallbrook District and people began homesteading shortly thereafter. Construction began on the railroad connecting Los Angeles to San Diego in 1881. The new line was extended to Fallbrook in 1882. A major flood washed out the tracks in 1884 and it took a year to get the line back in service. F.W. Bartlett and four adjacent homesteaders applied for a town designation under the State's Townsite Law in 1885, and what is today downtown Fallbrook was subdivided.

Few Victorian structures remain in the area. The Elder House was built in 1884 by Elmore Shipley and was remodeled numerous times. The front porch was undoubtedly added later, making it difficult to appreciate the lines of the original structure.

Elder House (1884) 127 West Elder Street

# VICTORIAN STYLES

Victorian is not a style; it defines a structure built in the time period of Queen Victoria's reign from 1837 to 1901. Victorian era houses in San Diego County were built in many styles, evolved from European and eastern United States designs. The houses constructed for the upper class were typically designed by architects and were more elaborate regardless of the underlying style. The houses built by middle and lower class residents were based upon commonly available design plans used by carpenters and were less ornate. Of the many architectural styles within the Victorian period, the ones described here are showcased in this book. Typical characteristics of these styles are listed, although it is common to find homes that display various elements from other styles, it is the dominant architectural features of a home that determine what style it is.

## SECOND EMPIRE (MANSARD) STYLE (1855-1885)
Mansard roof
Dormer windows
Patterned slate or wood shingles on roof
Cast iron or wood cresting
    above upper cornice
Classical pediments
Tall windows on first story

## ITALIANATE (1860-1888)
Rectangular massing
Low-pitched flat or hipped roof
Brackets/cornices
Paired and single windows
Tall, narrow windows
Square bay windows
Single-story porches
Hooded doors and window surrounds
Square tower or cupola
Corner boards
Multi-colored, paler tones,
    natural stone colors

## STICK STYLE (1860-1890)
Sharply pointed gables, steep pitched roof,
    multiple rooflines
Spindle work
Fans, sunbursts, and other decorative
    gable treatments
Vertical, horizontal, or diagonal
    exterior planking

Framing expressed on exterior
Projecting bays, gables and porches
Tall windows
Square bay windows and towers
Multi-colored, usually earth tones,
    natural colors

## EASTLAKE (1875-1890)
Decorative trusswork
Exposed half-timber framing
Intermingling of vertical and
    horizontal planes
Steeply pitched roofs, simple gables
Beaded spindles
Jigsaw wooden forms
Massive lathe-formed columns and
    balustrades

## QUEEN ANNE (1880-1900)
Irregular rooflines
Large projecting bay windows
Square, round or polygonal towers; turrets
Patterned shingles, especially for the gables
Porches, often multi-storied, often
    wrap-around or L-shaped
Decorative brackets and latticework
    on porches
Balconies with decorative brackets
    and latticework
Roof finials and crestings
Gable-roofed dormers

Cantilevered upper stories
Corbeled chimneys
Multi-colored, usually darker
    earth tones
Decorative bargeboards

## SHINGLE STYLE (1880-1900)
Shingle siding
Complex rooflines
Asymmetric forms
Wide porches
Narrow eaves
Broad gables
Curving eyebrow dormers
Shingle color typically darker tones
    barn red, dark green

## COLONIAL REVIVAL (1880-1940)
Symmetrical façade
Rectangular
Two to three stories
Brick or narrow wood siding
Simple, classical detailing
Gable roof
Pillars and columns
Multi-pane, double-hung windows
    with shutters
Dormers
Temple-like entrance: porticos
    topped by pediment

# Select Bibliography

Anonymous. "Bankers Hill Walking Tour." www.sandiegohistory.org/tours/bankertour. San Diego Historical Society, undated.

Anonymous. "Important Events in the City of San Diego's History." www.sandiego.gov/citizensassistance: May 16, 2007.

Anonymous. "National City's Gracious Victorian Homes." The Daily Transcript (January 29, 2003).

Anonymous. "Promenade Through the Past – A Brief History of Coronado and its Architectural Wonders." Coronado Historical Association, undated.

Anonymous. "The role of Valley Center in the history of early California." www.valleycenterhistory.org, April 11, 2007.

Anonymous. "Victorian Illustrated Architectural Dictionary." www.ah.bfn.org. July 22, 2007.

Baldwin, Debra Lee. "Time Warp – Victorian mansion is returned to its original glory." San Diego Home/Garden Lifestyles. September 2001, pp 76-86.

Bock, Gordon. "The Stick Style." Old House Journal Online. www.oldhousejournal.com/magazine. July 8, 2007.

Box Files. San Diego Historical Society Library and Manuscripts collection.

Chula Vista Historical Society. "Historic Chula Vista – Historic Homes and Other Historic Sites." Chula Vista Heritage Museum, 1997.

City of San Marcos. "San Marcos History." www.ci.san-marcos.ca.us, June 12, 2007.

Crane, Clare. "Matthew Sherman: Pioneer San Diegan." The Journal of San Diego History (Fall 1972, Volume 18, Number 4).

Department of Parks and Recreation. "Heritage Park." County of San Diego (December 1999).

Ewing, Nancy Hanks. Del Mar – Looking Back. Del Mar: self-published, 1998.

Flanigan, Kathleen, Susan H. Carrico, and Richard L. Carrico. "Oceanside, California's Pride – 1992 Cultural Resource Survey." City of Oceanside (March 3, 1993), pp 2.4-2.9.

Holmes, Deborah. "The Old House Web – Housing Styles." www.oldhouseweb.com/stories. July 8, 2007.

Howard-Jones, Marje. "Between Germany and Carlsbad: A High Yielding Bond." The Journal of San Diego History (Spring 1984, Volume 30, Number 2).

Johl, Karen. Timeless Treasures, San Diego's Victorian Heritage. San Diego, California: Rand Editions, 1982.

La Jolla Historical Society. "La Jolla: A Brief History." www.ljhs.org, June 13, 2007.

Lakeside Historical Society. "The Castle House." www.lakesidehistory.org: February 6, 2007.

La Mesa Historical Society. "History of La Mesa." www.lamesahistory.com: May 10, 2007.

Lemon Grove Historical Society. "The Allisons: Pioneer Land Speculators and Sheep Ranchers." The Lemon Tree (Spring 2005).

Moss, Andrea. "Preserving Poway's Properties." North County Times (June 31, 2005), p A-9.

Naverson, Kenneth. Beautiful America's California Victorians. Woodburn, Oregon: Beautiful America Publishing Company, 1998.

Taylor, David. "Victorian Houses – A Guide to the Major Architectural Styles." http://users.rcn.com/scndempr/dave/school.html: July 20, 2007.

Walter, Susan. "A Brief History of the Steins and the Stein Farm." www.thesteinfarm.org/history.htm

Whetstone, Margie L. "The Escondido Story." www.escondido.com. March 28, 2007.

# Acknowledgements

Wendy Barker, Executive Director, Escondido History Center

Cecilia Burr, Poway Historical and Memorial Society

Marilyn and Tom Carnes

Douglas and Kim Collier

Jonathan Ford, Visitor Center Manager, Coronado Museum of History and Art

George Franck, History Committee, North Park Community Association

John Fry, Pacific Beach Historical Society

Donna Golden, Local History Librarian, Chula Vista Public Library

Andrew Gordon, GIS Client Services Analyst, San Diego Association of Governments

Richard Greenbauer, Senior Planner, City of Oceanside

Susan Gutierrez, President, Carlsbad Historical Society
Joseph Harteis, County Assessor's Office, County of San Diego
Roy Hastings, City of San Marcos
Susan Heavilin
Sandra Holder, Community Development Director, City of Carlsbad
Katherine Hon, History Committee, North Park Community Association
Delores Johnson, Secretary, Historical Resources Board, City of San Diego
Gordon Jones, La Mesa Historical Society
Diane Kane, Senior Planner, Historical Resources Board, City of San Diego
Kristen La Grange, Estate Concierge, Britt Scripps Inn
Karen Lamphere, Principal Analyst, San Diego Association of
    Governments
Bob Leiter, Director of Land Use and Transportation Planning, San Diego
    Association of Governments
Corinne McCall
Ann McCaull, Associate Planner, City of Coronado
Ron Morrison, Mayor, City of National City
Cecelia Njust, Fallbrook Historical Society
Matthew Nye, Librarian, National City Public Library
Helen Ofield, President, Lemon Grove Historical Society
Harry Parashis
Craig Peters, Carlsbad Historical Society
Lori Anne Peoples & Christopher Pro
Jennifer Redmond, Editor-in-Chief, Sunbelt Publications
Aileen Reyes, Britt-Scripps Inn, 406 Maple Street
Roger Showley, Staff Writer, The San Diego Union Tribune
Nancy Smith, National City Living History Farm Preserve
Don Terwilliger, Del Mar Historical Society
Lynnette Tessitore-Lopez, Associate Planner, City of Chula Vista
Louise Torio & Steve Veach
Harriette Treadwell, Oceanside Historical Society
Susan Walter, National City Living History Farm Preserve - Stein Farm
Cindy Wassdorp, Realtor, Prudential California Realty
Nicolas Watson

## SPECIAL THANKS

Barbara Metzger who spent many hours editing the draft manuscript, greatly improving the final manuscript.

Sandé Lollis for painstakingly converting the original manuscript to the proper software for printing, and offering her professional expertise.

Bruce Coons for ensuring the historical accuracy of the book and helping to educate me in the differences between Victorian design styles.

Alana Coons for guiding me through the arduous publishing process, and for her attention to detail.

## NOTES

The location of the houses on page 2 are:
    Queen Anne #1 is in National City
    Italianate is in San Francisco
    Eastlake is in San Diego
    Queen Anne #2 and #3 are in Alameda